VENEZUELA

EXPLORE THE COUNTRIES

Big Buddy Books
An Imprint of Abdo Publishing
abdopublishing.com

Julie Murray

abdopublishing.com

Published by Abdo Publishing, a division of ABDO, PO Box 398166, Minneapolis, Minnesota 55439.
Copyright © 2018 by Abdo Consulting Group, Inc. International copyrights reserved in all countries. No part
of this book may be reproduced in any form without written permission from the publisher. Big Buddy Books™
is a trademark and logo of Abdo Publishing.

Printed in the United States of America, North Mankato, Minnesota.
052017
092017

Cover Photo: ©iStockphoto.com.
Interior Photos: ASSOCIATED PRESS (pp. 29, 31, 33); Granger, NYC — All rights reserved. (p. 13, 16);
   ©iStockphoto.com (pp. 5, 9, 11, 21, 23, 34, 35, 37, 38); M. Timothy O'Keefe/Alamy Stock Photo (p. 35);
   Prisma by Dukas Presseagentur GmbH/Alamy Stock Photo (p. 11); REUTERS/Alamy Stock Photo (p. 19);
   Ricardo Ribas/Alamy Stock Photo (p. 13); SPUTNIK/Alamy Stock Photo (p. 17); Keren Su/China Span/
   Alamy Stock Photo (p. 25); vario images GmbH & Co.KG/Alamy Stock Photo (p. 34); Jimmy Villalta/
   VWPics/Alamy Stock Photo (p. 15); Xinhua/Alamy Stock Photo (p. 27).

Coordinating Series Editor: Tamara L. Brittom
Editor: Katie Lajiness
Graphic Design: Taylor Higgins, Keely Mckernan

Country population and area figures taken from the CIA World Factbook.

Publisher's Cataloging-in-Publication Data

Names: Murray, Julie, 1969- , author.
Title: Venezuela / by Julie Murray.
Description: Minneapolis, MN : Abdo Publishing, 2018. | Series: Explore the
   countries | Includes bibliographical references and index.
Identifiers: LCCN 2016962355 | ISBN 9781532110542 (lib. bdg.) |
   ISBN 9781680788396 (ebook)
Subjects: LCSH: Venezuela--Juvenile literature.
Classification: DDC 987--dc23
LC record available at http://lccn.loc.gov/2016962355

VENEZUELA

CONTENTS

AROUND THE WORLD

Our world has many countries. Each country has beautiful land. It has its own rich history. And, the people have their own languages and ways of life.

Venezuela is a country in South America. What do you know about Venezuela? Let's learn more about this place and its story!

Did You Know?

Spanish is the official language in Venezuela.

The National Pantheon of Venezuela honors those who fought for the country throughout history.

PASSPORT TO VENEZUELA

Venezuela is in the northern part of South America. Various islands in the Caribbean also belong to Venezuela. Brazil, Colombia, and Guyana share borders with Venezuela. The Caribbean Sea is to the north.

The country's total area is 352,144 square miles (912,049 sq km). Nearly 31 million people live in Venezuela.

SAY IT

Venezuela
veh-nuh-ZWAY-luh

WHERE IN THE WORLD?

Caribbean Sea

VENEZUELA

COLOMBIA

GUYANA

BRAZIL

Did You Know?

Venezuela is twice the size of California.

IMPORTANT CITIES

Caracas is Venezuela's **capital** and largest city. Almost 3 million people call it home. The city was founded in 1567. During the 1940s, the oil industry helped it grow quickly.

Over time, Caracas became the center of the country's **economy**. The city has many large manufacturing businesses. They produce cleansers, paper products, rubber, and clothes. Caracas is also home to banking and service companies.

SAY IT

Caracas
kah-RAH-kahs

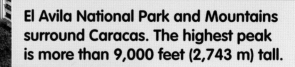

El Avila National Park and Mountains surround Caracas. The highest peak is more than 9,000 feet (2,743 m) tall.

Maracaibo is Venezuela's second-largest city. It has a little more than 2 million citizens. In the beginning, the city was famous for its coffee. Then oil was discovered and the **economy** boomed. Today, Maracaibo is also home to one of the country's most important ports.

Venezuela's third-largest city is Valencia. About 1.7 million people live there. In 1812 and 1830, Valencia served as the **capital** of Venezuela. Animal feed, cars, clothes, plastics, soaps, and tires are produced there. Its factories process cotton, coffee, and sugarcane.

Lake Maracaibo is the largest natural lake in South America. It covers 5,130 square miles (13,287 sq km).

SAY IT

Maracaibo
ma-ruh-KEYE-boh

Valencia
vuh-LEHN-shee-uh

Built in 1976, Altar de la Patria honors the battle that freed Venezuela from Spain.

Venezuela in History

For thousands of years, native tribes lived in what is now Venezuela. In 1498, Spanish **explorers** discovered the area. For nearly 300 years, Spain ruled over the land and its people.

In 1819, Venezuela became part of Gran Colombia. This area included what is now Colombia, Ecuador, Panama, and Venezuela. In 1830, Venezuela became an independent country.

Explorers visiting what is now Venezuela saw houses built on stilts. They named the land Venezuela, which means Little Venice.

Simon Bolivar was a leader who helped free Venezuela from Spain.

After gaining independence, the Venezuelan people continued to fight for freedom. For decades, the people held **riots**. They protested different **dictators**. After 1935, new political parties were created. Since 1958, all Venezuelan presidents have been elected by popular vote.

The people of Venezuela have had many struggles. In 1999, floods and mudslides killed about 30,000 people. Since 2015, many Venezuelans have struggled with a weak **economy**.

In Caracas, the poorest people live in slums. Many live in houses made of plywood, metal, plastic, and cardboard. These areas do not have clean water or electricity.

Timeline

1498–1499

Explorers Christopher Columbus and Alonso de Ojeda visited Venezuela.

1521

The Spanish turned Venezuela into a **colony**.

1811

The Act of Independence was signed. This set the country free from Spain's control.

1829–1830

Venezuela became an independent **republic** with its **capital** in Caracas.

1998

Hugo Chavez was elected president. He ruled until his death in 2013.

2016

Thousands of people **rioted** over a lack of food.

AN IMPORTANT SYMBOL

Venezuela's flag has three stripes. They are yellow, blue, and red. Eight white stars are in the middle. The country's **coat of arms** is on the yellow stripe.

The country is a **federal republic**. The president is the head of government.

Venezuela is divided into 23 states. Each state has its own elected officials.

SAY IT

Nicolás Maduro
NIH-kuh-laws MAD-uhr-oh

The modern Venezuelan flag was adopted in 2006.

Nicolás Maduro was elected president in 2013. In Venezuela, presidents can serve unlimited six-year terms.

Across the Land

Venezuela has a diverse landscape with jungles, mountains, and valleys. Many rivers run though the country. The Orinoco River is Venezuela's largest river. It is 1,700 miles (2,736 km) long.

Did You Know?

The average temperature is 83°F (28°C) in central and northern Venezuela. In the mountains, the temperature averages 67°F (19°C).

The Orinoco River runs from the Guiana Highlands to the Atlantic Ocean.

Forests cover half of Venezuela. And, grasslands cover the other half. In the southern part of the country, rainforests provide homes for many different animals.

Jaguars and other wildcats are in Venezuela's forests. Bears, deer, monkeys, and skunks are also nearby. Alligators, lizards, and turtles live in rivers and swamps. Many birds such as parrots, ducks, and herons also live in these swamps.

Part of the Amazon Rainforest is in Venezuela. About 10 percent of the world's animal species live there.

In Venezuela, the number of jaguars continues to go down. So, hunting jaguars is illegal.

23

Earning a Living

Oil and natural gas make up much of Venezuela's **economy**. The area's **natural resources** include coal, diamond, gold, and iron ore.

Many people work in factories. They produce aluminum, clothes, iron, and steel. Others have banking and service jobs.

Farming is a small part of the economy. The main crops include bananas, corn, rice, and sugarcane. Many farmers raise cattle in the grasslands.

Venezuela's oil refinery is one of the largest in the world. In 2016, Venezuela produced about 2 million barrels of oil per day.

LIFE IN VENEZUELA

Carnival is a popular holiday in Venezuela. Every February, people hold parades, play games, and party in the streets.

Food is an important part of Venezuelan society. Common foods include black beans, a type of banana called plantains, and rice. Many kinds of meat are cooked as part of their meals.

Carnival is held 40 days before Easter. The Spanish brought this Catholic tradition to Venezuela.

Venezuela still practices *toros coleados,* a form of bullfighting. Many enjoy baseball and soccer. Adventure-seekers kayak down the Orinoco River. And, some climb or ski on the mountain ranges.

Most people in Venezuela are **Catholic**. They celebrate holidays such as Christmas and Easter. Smaller groups of Venezuelans follow other religions.

Did You Know?

In Venezuela, children from ages 6 to 15 must attend school. Venezuelans receive a free education from kindergarten through graduate school.

In 2016, Venezuela played Uruguay in the America Cup soccer championship. Venezuela won with a score of 1 to 0.

FAMOUS FACES

Many talented people are from Venezuela. Carolina Herrera is a clothing **designer**. She was born on January 8, 1939, in Caracas.

In 1981, Herrera started a clothing company in New York City, New York. Soon, famous women began to wear her clothes. Today, her line includes perfumes and men's clothes, among other collections.

Herrera never studied fashion in school. She had natural talent, so her designs always looked beautiful.

Hugo Chavez was president of Venezuela. He was born on July 28, 1954, in Sabaneta, Venezuela. Chavez started out in the army. He became unhappy with the government. So, he tried to take it over in 1992. Chavez was arrested and went to prison until 1994.

After his release, Chavez started a new political party. In 1998, he ran for president of Venezuela. Chavez served as president from 1999 to 2013. During those years, his ideas created a deeply divided country. Chavez died on March 5, 2013, in Caracas.

Chavez (*left*) had a close friendship with Fidel Castro (*right*), the dictator of Cuba. They shared ideas that many other leaders did not agree with.

TOUR BOOK

Imagine traveling to Venezuela! Here are some places you could go and things you could do.

Ride

The cable car in Mérida is the world's highest. It is 15,633 feet (4,765 m) high and runs almost 8 miles (13 km).

Explore

Coro is an early colonial village near the Caribbean coast. See more than 600 historic buildings.

 Hike

The Amazon Rainforest receives more than 100 inches (254 cm) of rain per year.

 Discover

At 3,212 feet (979 m) high, Angel Falls is the world's highest waterfall.

Swim

Margarita's Island is Venezuela's largest Caribbean island. Walk on the shore and swim in the Caribbean Sea.

A GREAT COUNTRY

The story of Venezuela is important to our world. Venezuela is a land of mountains and jungles. It is a country of people with strong beliefs.

The people and places that make up Venezuela offer something special. They help make the world a more beautiful, interesting place.

Mount Roraima can only be reached by a three-day hike. Every year, thousands of people travel there.

Venezuela Up Close

Official Name:
Bolivarian Republic of Venezuela

Flag:

Population (rank): 30,912,302
(July 2016 est.)
(43rd most-populated country)

Total Area (rank): 352,144 square miles
(33rd largest country)

Capital: Caracas

Official Language: Spanish

Currency: Venezuelan bolivar

Form of Government: Federal republic

National Anthem: "Gloria al Bravo Pueblo"
("Glory to the Brave People")

IMPORTANT WORDS

capital a city where government leaders meet.

Catholic a member of the Roman Catholic Church. This kind of Christianity has been around since the first century and is led by the pope.

coat of arms a shield or other surface bearing symbols or words. These represent a country's history and accomplishments.

colony land settled by people from another area.

designer (dih-ZEYE-nuhr) someone who has ideas and works on making a plan.

dictator a ruler with complete control.

economy the way that a country produces, sells, and buys goods and services.

explorer a person who travels to new, or unknown places.

federal republic a form of government in which the people choose the leader. The central government and the individual states share power.

natural resources useful and valued supplies from nature.

republic a government in which the people choose the leader.

riot a situation in which a large group of people behaves in a violent and uncontrolled way.

WEBSITES

To learn more about Explore the Countries, visit **abdobooklinks.com**. These links are routinely monitored and updated to provide the most current information available.

INDEX